What Happens in Fall?

Apples in Fall

by Mari Schuh

Ideas for Parents and Teachers

Bullfrog Books let children practice reading informational text at the earliest reading levels. Repetition, familiar words, and photo labels support early readers.

Before Reading
- Discuss the cover photo. What does it tell them?
- Look at the picture glossary together. Read and discuss the words.

Read the Book
- "Walk" through the book and look at the photos. Let the child ask questions. Point out the photo labels.
- Read the book to the child, or have him or her read independently.

After Reading
- Prompt the child to think more. Ask: Do you eat apples in fall? Which kind is your favorite? How do you like to eat them?

The author dedicates this book to Isla McGinnis of Racine, Wisconsin.

Bullfrog Books are published by Jump!
5357 Penn Avenue South
Minneapolis, MN 55419
www.jumplibrary.com

Library of Congress Cataloging-in-Publication Data
Schuh, Mari C., 1975-
  Apples in fall / by Mari Schuh.
    p. cm. — (Bullfrog books. What happens in fall?)
  Audience: 5.
  Audience: K to grade 3.
  Summary: "Visit an apple orchard and learn how apples grow, how cider is made, and what foods we make with apples. Color photos and easy-to-read text tell about this favorite treat in the season of fall" —Provided by publisher.
  Includes bibliographical references and index.
  ISBN 978-1-62031-057-1 (hardcover : alk. paper) — ISBN 978-1-62496-075-8 (ebook)
  1. Apples—Juvenile literature. 2. Apples—Harvesting—Juvenile literature. 3. Autumn—Juvenile literature. I. Title.
  SB363.S384 2014
  634'.11—dc23
                                    2013001947

Series Editor: Rebecca Glaser
Series Designer: Ellen Huber
Book Designer: Heather Dreisbach
Photo Researcher: Heather Dreisbach

Photo Credits:
All photos from Shutterstock except: Dreamstime, 4, 21; Superstock, 6–7, 9, 11, 15

Printed in the United States of America at Corporate Graphics, in North Mankato, Minnesota.
5-2013 / PO 1003
10 9 8 7 6 5 4 3 2 1

Table of Contents

At the Orchard

Today is a fall day.

Let's go to
the orchard.

The trees are full of apples.

The apples grew all summer.

They are ripe in fall.

press

Workers make apple cider.
First they mash the apples.
Then a big press
squeezes down.
Cider comes out. Yum!

Dad tastes many apples.
He likes Gala apples best.
They are sweet.

Mom buys Granny
Smith apples.

They are big
and green.

She buys
two bags.

At home, Pam cooks her apples.

She makes ten jars of applesauce.

15

Sue peels and cuts her apples.

She adds sugar, flour, and butter.

What will it be?

Apple pie!

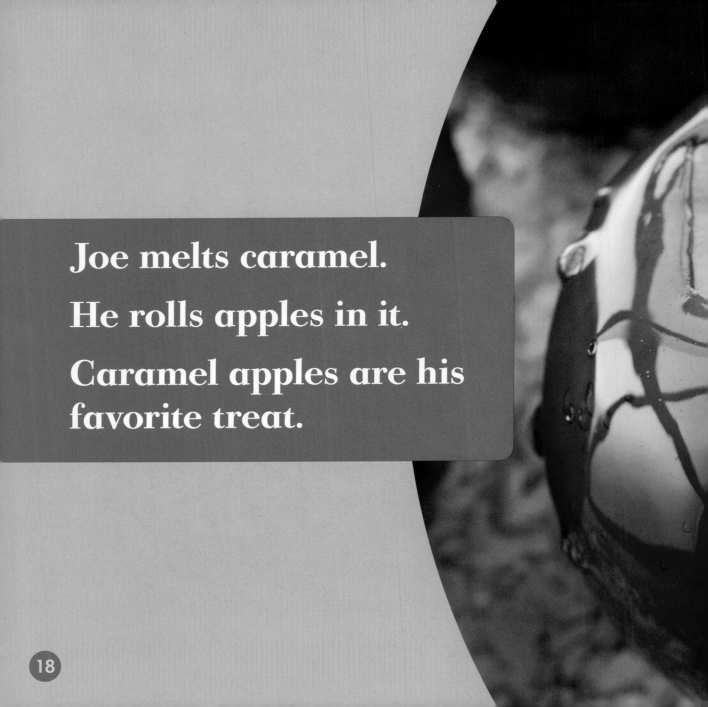

Joe melts caramel.

He rolls apples in it.

Caramel apples are his favorite treat.

Crunch!

How do you eat apples?

Parts of an Apple

stem
The part of the fruit that attaches to the apple tree.

flesh
The white inside of an apple that people eat.

seeds
The part that can grow more apple trees.

core
The center of the apple that holds the seeds.

skin
The apple's waxy covering that contains many vitamins.

Picture Glossary

caramel
A smooth, chewy candy.

orchard
An area where fruit trees are grown.

cider
A drink made from mashed apples.

press
A strong machine that uses force; some presses are used to make apple cider.

Index

To Learn More

Learning more is as easy as 1, 2, 3.

1) Go to www.factsurfer.com

2) Enter "apple" into the search box.

3) Click the "Surf" button to see a list of websites.

With factsurfer.com, finding more information is just a click away.